# *Seeds to Happiness*

Shift to a Higher Perspective and
Follow Your Dreams

AVA MUCIKYAN

**BALBOA.**PRESS
A DIVISION OF HAY HOUSE

Balboa Press books may be ordered through booksellers or by contacting:

Balboa Press
A Division of Hay House
1663 Liberty Drive
Bloomington, IN 47403
www.balboapress.com
844-682-1282

Print information available on the last page.

ISBN: 978-1-9822-5463-6 (sc)
ISBN: 978-1-9822-5464-3 (e)

Balboa Press rev. date: 10/28/2020

# Seeds to Happiness

*Dedication*

*This book is dedicated to my son Ethan, who is wiser and more compassionate than anyone I know. He is the one person who holds me accountable to strive to be the better version of myself each and every day.*

# Table of Contents

## Introduction

Welcome to *Seeds to Happiness*................................xi

My Journey to a Higher Perspective ....................xiii

How to Use this Book......................................xix

## The Seeds to Happiness

### Guiding Principle #1 – Claim Your Dream
### Your Power, Passion, and Purpose

I Have a Dream….....................................1

Embrace & Heal Your Inner Child.................3

Standards Baby….........................................5

Your Purpose Is Bigger Than You ..................7

### Guiding Principle #2 – Walk the Path to
### Your Dream

You Are the Star and the
Playwright of Your Own Movie.....................11

Happily Ever After Starts with a Choice ......15

The Grace of Courage................................17

Tears Are Your Superpower ........................19

Life Is a Balance of Holding On and Letting Go….......21

Mirror, Mirror on the Wall…....................25

A Grateful Heart Is a Magnet for Miracles ..................29

Tune-In to Abundance Mindset .....................33

Energy Is Our Currency...............................35

## Guiding Principle #3 – Starve Your Fears & Limiting Beliefs

Conquer Your Fears......................................................39

Restructure Your Beliefs to Create the Life You Want...43

Follow Your Passion Blindly – You ARE Enough ........47

You Can't Do Life Alone ...............................................51

The Only Way to It, Is Through It...............................55

Breaking the Chains of Codependency.......................57

## Guiding Principle #4 – Embrace Love as You Chase Your Dreams

The Art of Self-Care ....................................................61

Love Is an Inside Job ...................................................65

Open Your Heart to Settle Your Mind.........................69

If $Money$ Wasn't an Issue

What Would You Be Doing? ........................................73

The Sky Is the Limit ....................................................75

## Conclusion................................................................79

## Afterword .................................................................81

## Acknowledgments.....................................................85

# Introduction

## Welcome to *Seeds to Happiness*

Thank you for answering the call to pick up this book. Something is stirring in you, a resonance with the idea of knowing what seeds of wisdom will lead to living life from a higher perspective.

Often times our perspective tends to narrow to tunnel vision as we face life's challenges. With dark clouds hovering over our head, the light at the end of the tunnel is hard to see. We need to assess the situation from another perspective, a higher perspective. When we are feeling stressed, anxious, or rushed, we can't think clearly. Our energy vibration lowers, and we get caught up in our little box of fears.

Generally, there are a few main reasons for this:

- ☐ We are blinded by our ego and pride
- ☐ We are too caught up in our emotions
- ☐ We are looking at things too closely – as if with a magnifying glass
- ☐ We are feeling pressured to resolve things too quickly
- ☐ We are biased in our opinions
- ☐ We cannot tell the difference between our gut feeling and our sabotaging thoughts

However, once we learn how to rise above our isolated situation, we can see at least five ways out of our situation, which were unavailable until we tuned into a higher perspective.

Throughout this book, I will be talking about different themes, from the power of self-love and self-worth to ways to care for yourself and break dysfunctional patterns. I'll do my best to give you a higher perspective on things from my personal experiences and research. This perspective will allow you to see the situations you are in from above, not below, and to help you make clearer choices out of compassion and love, instead of fear or ego.

# My Journey to a Higher Perspective

Growing up as a child of a single mother in the Soviet Regime, I could feel that regime everywhere, including our household. My mother was a Ph.D. Professor of Economics, and I was a little feisty tomboy with a sharp tongue who was fluent in sarcasm and jokes. I was a fearless little one.

Being raised by such a strict mother was not an easy task for an adventurer like myself. Knowing I would be denied before ever asking, I always had at least three ways I was going to get my way anyway. This created the optimist rule breaker in me. I weighed my punishments against the reward of the adventures and was prepared for the consequences.

I had a low tolerance for things that didn't interest me. My motto has always been - *if it's not fun, it's not worth doing it* – and by fun I don't just mean entertaining. Even hard work had to be wired with some kind of passion behind it.

My mom took me traveling almost every year, and I believe that is an important part of human growth. It takes you out of your little box and helps you see cultures and people that are unlike you. This led me coming to the United States at the age of 18, to participate in an academic exchange program. It was a life-altering year for me and I returned home a different person.

I never felt a sense of fully belonging to any place or group after my student exchange program. By category, I was White, but I felt nothing White - my culture is a good mix of Hispanic and Black cultures, and my strict upbringing reminds me of the Asian culture. After graduating from the University in Armenia and working a few years, I felt the itch to get back to States. I couldn't fit back into my own culture. The hierarchy of men and women, the post-Soviet regime, and the internal tensions were too intense. I felt like the walls were closing in on me. I made a commitment to myself to make it my mission to make a change. I decided to continue my education and obtain my Master's Degree from the American University in Washington, D.C. In August of 2005, I packed my suitcase and the $800 I had saved, and ventured out on a life-long journey. I had no idea where I was going to stay or how I was going to cover my living expenses, but I was sure I would figure it out. And I did.

After graduation, I spent the next 10 years of my life building a family, getting a career, and chasing titles. I thought life was complete. What more could you ask for, right? I had a "Facebook perfect" family, a beautiful house, five investment homes, a six-figure salary and a VP title at one of the major banks in the nation. My mother had even moved from Armenia to help me with my child. I really thought I'd made it in this thing called LIFE. On the surface I had everything a girl could ever ask for, but underneath the carpet was slipping away and things were about to take a very different turn for me.

Within a few months after I had my son, my marriage fell apart and I lost the six-figure salary that winter. Christmas was not very merry for our family that year. I had an emotional breakdown. I couldn't figure out where I had gone wrong in life, and all I could come up with was *I AM NOT GOOD ENOUGH*.

Instead of taking time to look within, I did what a traditional tough girl should do. I suppressed my emotions for the sake of my child, ignored the situation to save my family, and decided to start a business to bury myself in more work.

Over the next few years all I did was work. I numbed myself to everything and felt like a robot bulldozer who only knew how to push forward. Until I finally broke down ... again. This time I had a successful business, but I was empty on the inside, exhausted on the outside, feeling like a failure as a mother, and at a dead end within my marriage.

The next few years were a blur. I left everything behind and started soul searching, contemplating, meditating, and taking it day by day. The flood gates opened and I started feeling everything I had suppressed for years. The journey to self-discovery and healing was a long one. But in the end, I am grateful for the strength and divine guidance to have withstood the storm. It gave me wisdom and knowledge to awaken to my purpose, and from that pain I birthed this book.

The Salt Room was a result of transmuted pain and pressure. I was looking for an outlet to feed my soul. It provided everything I needed to heal and restore my mind, body, and spirit connection. I realized that all that energy I had put into creating The Salt Room drew people in that also needed to heal.

The Salt Room Las Vegas is a wellness center that helps

guests connect with their mind, body and spirit. It uses the healing powers of Himalayan salt to relieve a list of respiratory and skin conditions, provides deep relaxation for the mind, and offers conventional services, such as massages, facials, yoga & meditation classes.

Slowly, I started getting to know myself, relearning my passion, and bringing back the feisty little tomboy that had big dreams of changing the world. I started to see life from a higher perspective. I realized that my passion for helping women feel empowered and follow their dreams was directly correlated to the most painful part of my journey.

Everything starts with self-care! People who walk through my doors have already committed to that first important step. Loving and taking care of self is a crucial part of making a change in the world. When your love tank is full, it overflows to everyone around you. The Salt Room helps men and women connect with their mind, body and spirit, which is why my customers call it their "Happy Place." Once they take care of themselves, they can't help but spread that positivity all around them.

Reflecting back on my journey, I can say one thing that kept me on track was following my heart. Every bold decision was wired with a passion so strong that nothing and no one could change my mind. I have always lived life to the fullest. Even with the ups and rock bottom downs, I went all in. If I had to do it again, I wouldn't change a thing. My journey of empowerment is only starting. The dreamer girl is still in me and the best is yet to come.

I invite every one of you to live life boldly and to the fullest, to plant your own seeds to happiness, become the best version of yourself and live life from a higher perspective!

# How to Use this Book

I wrote the *Seeds to Happiness* as individual blog posts over the course of a year. Each one came pouring out of me and felt very effortless. When I decided to put the blog posts together as a collection, I loosely organized them by topic. Here are my suggestions for how to enjoy and cultivate these nuggets of wisdom that guided me to a higher perspective.

☐ Read what calls to you. I know I can't change you. Only you can change you. But, I can plant a seed of awareness.

☐ Find a way to record your thoughts & reflections. Get a notebook or a journal, use your phone notes, or a laptop if you prefer.

☐ Once you know the truth, you can't go back to unknowing. Choose to take the scales off and see the truth; shed what is no longer serving you.

☐ Make daily choices to give yourself time to read a portion of the book and reflect on how the seeds are showing up in your life.

☐ Allow the guiding principles to become second nature for you. Once this happens, you will know that these tools and strategies are there for you to return to as needed.

☐ Recognize there are seasons for growth and learning, for creative endeavors, and also for business development.

You may find yourself in a powerful growth spurt for several months, and afterwards you may enter an entrepreneurial phase. That is fine. Just develop your daily practices that will always ground you back into your truth.

The seeds are doing their job if they open you up and guide you to develop a daily routine to feed your happiness and well-being. It is important to incorporate spiritual, physical and nutritional routines for achieving a balanced life. I will share with you what helped me during the darkest time of my life, when energy ran low and it seemed impossible to see the light at the end of the tunnel. Please realize the results may not be instant, so consistency is key.

# Guiding Principle # 1

*Claim Your Dream*
*Your Power, Passion, and Purpose*

# I Have a Dream...

*Time doesn't wait. Indecision will only let opportunities slip by. Pick a path and walk confidently with your heart behind every step.* – Doe Zantamata

I HAVE A DREAM! A BIG DREAM! A dream that one day, all the women in the world will finally understand their worth, unlock their potential, release all their fears, and GO CHASE THEIR BIG DREAMS. How am I going to achieve this? I have no idea. But I do know this, as long as my standards of integrity align with my mission, every step I take is going to have this dream in mind. Every chance I get to speak to a woman, I plant a seed of inspiration and lift them up to the best of my abilities; every opportunity I get to purchase something I try to support a woman-owned business. These small initiatives are backed by big dreams and it is my honor to support those dreams.

I may not have a magic wand to wave and cast a spell, but that doesn't mean I can't start small. Who would have ever thought that ten years ago we would have these little devices in our hands that are capable of spreading news with lightning speed across the world? So maybe very soon I will get a hold of my "magic wand." But for now, even inspiring one person a day is most fulfilling for me.

Find your purpose. Find that one thing that makes your

eyes shine, your voice shake, and fills your heart. There is your purpose and you need to pursue it. Think big. Your purpose is not necessarily what you like to do, but the intention behind why you are doing it. Keep asking yourself why do I like what I like? Why do I do what I do? Dig deep, get comfortable with why until you find the root of your passion, which will lead you to your purpose.

So take a step, a tiny step, but do it now. Have no fear as you'll be guided. Trust yourself and trust your inner wisdom. You have a purpose that is bigger than you, and it is not negotiable. There are people who are waiting for what you have to offer to them. You don't have to have everything figured out or have all your ducks in a row. Take a step and ducks will line up on their own. For as long as your heart beats and your belly breathes, YOU HAVE A PURPOSE TO FULFILL.

# Embrace & Heal Your Inner Child

*Every child is an artist. The problem is how
to remain an artist once we grow up.*
– Pablo Picasso

As children we are very in touch with our feelings and emotions. We know what we want and we are not scared to go for it. We rarely overthink a situation and are always honest and straightforward with our wants and needs. As children we are also more creative, more compassionate, more forgiving, and more patient with ourselves and others. We are dreamers …

So what happens? How do we lose touch with ourselves? At what point do we lose our compassion towards ourselves and others, lose our creativity and imagination and start limiting ourselves to conform and please? As children we are not worried about being wrong or breaking rules. As we mature we quickly learn that being wrong often has negative consequences. At school, we're penalized for being wrong. At work, we're penalized for being wrong, even at home we're penalized for being wrong. According to Sir Ken Robinson, an expert in creativity, "If you're not prepared to be wrong, you'll never come up with anything original." Social norms and religions have done a wonderful job conforming us into perfect soldiers that comply and abide by the rules. We are being conditioned and limited in our imagination, dreams, and creativity, and slowly becoming dependent on their instructions of right or wrong. The result? Lost sense of self!

At some point we become aware that the reality we live in is not satisfying. Hopefully sooner rather than later we connect with our inner child and begin the search. Let's spend some time getting to know ourselves. Break old patterns and rules, be fearless, try new things - just go for it. Unlock the courage and conquer your fears, think with your hearts and ignore the mind.

If it feels good – do it. If it doesn't – don't. Trust yourself. You have all the answers inside of you, you do not need anyone to guide you or give you a road map to success and happiness. You are enough!

# Standards Baby...

*Happiness is when what you think, what you*
*say, and what you do are in harmony.*
– Gandhi

I am not just talking about having standards for men/women, items you buy, or hotels you stay at, but rather more like having a BLUEPRINT FOR LIFE. Spend some time crafting your blueprint for life, then walk the talk. Crafting your personal standards of integrity will help you define your core values and live your life unapologetically.

Well, how do I create my standards you might wonder?

Step 1 - Connect with your true self and figure out what makes you happy and gives you joy. Not people around you, not your child, not your family, but YOU. What do you like and what do you dislike? Make sure the WHY comes from your authentic self - the inner child of yours, not the you that is filled with societal programming and is worried about other people's opinions. Really spend some time to get to know yourself. The best way to start is to weed out things that you don't like. Let your intuition be your guide and your heart be your navigation system. Don't forget to actually make a list of everything that makes you happy and brings you joy.

Step 2 - Write a list of all the people you admire - teachers, neighbors, celebrities and influencers. Then identify the personality features you admire about each person. Take a minute to read each one of these qualities out loud and pay attention how it makes you feel. Write down the qualities and traits that resonate. These are qualities that reside within you, and you need to connect with them.

Congratulations, you have officially established your standards of integrity. Now if you take these standards and add the choices based on these standards while keeping your dream in mind, it will give you the shortest and straightest path to your dream!

Alternatively, when you deviate from your own standards, or make choices disregarding them, you violate your own integrity resulting in an energy drain. Guilt, resentment, regret, and remorse start creeping in to sidetrack you. Don't worry. Each day is a new slate. So next time you are presented with a choice, ask yourself:

1. Is this in line with my standards of integrity?
2. Is this in line with my dream/purpose?
3. Does this bring me joy or happiness?

By simply answering these questions you should be able to make an educated decision. Harness your energy by living your blueprint and it will keep you on track and help fuel your dreams.

# Your Purpose Is Bigger Than You

*The basis of your life is freedom, the purpose
of your life is joy.* – Abraham Hicks

You can't run away from your destiny. Sound familiar? Well it's true. If you try to, you'll be miserable and completely out of alignment, doing unfulfilling things you don't love to do and wasting precious days moving farther away from yourself. On the contrary, when you tune into your purpose, you plug into your matrix. Synchronicities amplify, déjà vu's become more frequent, and all of this is simply your confirmation that you are on the right path.

When you finally get back on your rails and stop hustling off the tracks (which could be very painful – imagine a train driving off the tracks), magical things happen. You feel a sudden rush of energy flowing through your system. You feel motivated, happy, and excited. You find yourself surrounded by people who share your vision, who finish your sentences, and complete your thoughts. It's almost like a breath of fresh air and an affirmation that you are neither crazy nor alone. Once you align, life flows easier, the wind of success just picks you up and effortlessly pushes you forward towards manifesting your dreams.

We usually call it catching a wave or a streak of luck. What we fail to recognize is that a wave does not have to stop.

Yes, there are always dips in our journey, but if you are fully tuned into your matrix, you easily identify and learn from the lessons and move right on. It's almost surreal how such a simple realization can take us sometimes decades to understand.

So how do we tune into our purpose?

1.  Nurture your dreams and work on them regularly at whatever stage you may be. Create a plan and start with the end in mind. Break it down into bite size achievable goals and work on it daily.
2.  Stay flexible to change. You'll notice throughout your journey things will shift and change. Make necessary adjustments to your process to stay in flow. Instead of doubting yourself check back with your standards of integrity (Re-read *Standards Baby*).
3.  Stay focused. Remember, in life it's easy to get caught up in your daily drama and start looking at things with a magnifying glass. Instead, from time to time, distance yourself from it. Look at your journey from a bird's eye view – where you are, where you came from, and where are you going. Then go back to the original dream and make the necessary adjustments.
4.  Remember when you get stuck - you are NOT alone. There is plenty of help around if you just reach out and ask for it. Identify your issues, and instead of staying stuck in the problem, look for solutions. As long as you are searching, you will be guided to find your answers.

# Guiding Principle #2

## *Walk the Path to Your Dream*

# You Are the Star and the Playwright of Your Own Movie

*All the world's a stage, and all the men and women merely players.* – William Shakespeare

Most of you have heard about this quote by Shakespeare, but have you really thought about it? Nothing in life is happening TO you – everything is happening BY you and THROUGH you. Every situation in your life is a scene waiting to unfold and everyone that crosses your path is also an actor that has a role in your life. Just this one perspective shift alone can change your view and your reaction to life.

Some people cross your path to change your direction, some people are strategically placed in your life to wreck your boat. The important thing to remember is avoid getting caught up in the blame game. Understand there is a very good reason that s/he happened to play the role of the 'bad guy' in your life. Don't shoot the messenger!

If you just tune in well enough, you will see the magical purpose of each encounter. Look back at your life and you will notice you have always gotten what you wanted. The process of getting to your goal may not have always been as you envisioned it, but the end result is always what you wished for. This is because not only are you the star of your movie but you are also the playwright. You create your reality with your thoughts, and what you focus on manifests.

When you make a wish, the entire Universe conspires to make it happen for you. From the point of conception to the end, every situation and encounter is geared towards preparing and equipping you with necessary skills to achieve your end goal. Our main problem is that we like to be in control of the process (or think we are). What we fail to realize is that we don't have the capacity to manifest things as precisely as the Universe does. We get caught up in our dramas and expectations, creating unnecessary negativity (resentment, anger, frustration) and forgetting that everything is in divine order.

Once the goal is accomplished and you are able to look back, you see that every situation and every encounter, every lesson and every painful moment was necessary in order to gain the wisdom, the strength, and the skills to achieve your original goal. So …

- ☐ Make sure you are creating a movie that you'd like to star in
- ☐ Get excited about all the scenes in your movie
- ☐ Stop the negativity by keeping the end result in mind
- ☐ Surrender control, keep the faith, and trust the process
- ☐ Gear up with patience and buckle up
- ☐ Get some popcorn, sit back, and enjoy the show

When you carry regrets, guilt, and other heavy emotions along with you, they play in your mind like an old record player, and prevent you from living your life to the fullest. Rewriting the scripts and accepting the current situation as it is allows you to move on with your life.

# Happily Ever After Starts with a Choice

*"This present moment. That lives on. To become. Long ago."* – Gary Snyder

Life is comprised of moments, which turn into days, which then turn into months and years that eventually come to comprise your whole life. Every morning when you wake up you make tiny little decisions that have great power over your entire life. What's the first thing that crosses your mind? Is it positive or negative? If it is negative, it is your choice to consciously switch that one thought into a positive one and see a blessing in that particular moment. During breakfast you have the choice of having a bagel or a smoothie, which one would you choose to nourish your body? Again, seems like a simple, innocent choice, yet consistently choosing the bagel will have long-term health consequences.

Someone angers you at work, what do you do? Respond with anger or chose to not react out of impulse? By responding out of emotion, you feed the negativity while you have the power to stop it from spreading. Similarly, every moment during the day you have a choice. Those little choices are what make your day a bad day or a great day. And one day this moment will become your long ago, the moment you'd like to remember with a smile.

Every choice you make, whether big or small, has

consequences. Think of how many events in history could have been prevented had humanity made a conscious loving choice. Regardless of cultures and religions, every human in this world knows the language of love and kindness. We are all hardwired with consciousness and compassion. Sure, every choice has consequences, but most importantly, you are the one who has to live with the long-term consequences of every little choice you make. It is that simple – just make conscious choices, practice the pause, and always ask yourself if this is the choice fueled with love and kindness or is the underlying temporary emotion trying to push you to act on an impulse? Always choose to stay in your power and always choose LOVE.

# The Grace of Courage

*Having a soft heart in a cruel world is not weakness, it's courage.–* Katherine Henson

Did you know that the original Latin meaning for the word "courage" is heart? I think there is a deeper reason for it that got lost overtime. Courage is not the ability to hold it all together and be tough, but the ability to show up and let yourself be seen, as Brené Brown puts it. The real courage is to be soft, loving, and forgiving. That is true strength of the heart.

As children we are very in touch with our feelings and emotions; we are all born with lots of love and compassion in our hearts. Regardless what hand we were dealt, our love was unconditional. We were all born as soft gentle souls, but somewhere along the way we were convinced that softness is a weakness, unconditional love gets us hurt, and sensitive people can't survive this harsh world. So we started running away from it and chose to join the majority in order to fit in.

You have a choice today to have the courage to yield to your soft soul and understand that you can only heal with love. Have the courage to let go of all anger, frustration, jealousy or any other low vibration emotion, and elevate above your circumstances. You will then find your inner wisdom to see the bigger picture of life, find your inner calling, and surrender to the flow of life with grace. And remember, hard and stiff is bound to break eventually. Have the courage to be soft and flexible again, and you will liberate your soul.

# Tears Are Your Superpower

*There is a sacredness in tears. They are not a mark of weakness,
but of power. They speak more eloquently than ten thousand
tongues. They are the messengers of overwhelming grief, of deep
contrition and of unspeakable love.* – Washington Irving

Tears are my superpower, what's yours?! Why do we tend to
suppress something that is so natural to our human nature? Why
is there so much stigma around an instinct? Somehow happy
tears are good, but tears of sadness are a sign of weakness. Who
invented this? Tears are the body's natural release mechanism,
just like laughing. They are healing and stress relieving. In
fact, they are a sign of courage, strength, and authenticity.
Emotional tears have health benefits. Typically, after crying, we
release emotional toxins, our breathing and heart rate decrease,
and we enter into a calmer biological and emotional state.

Let go of the old programming that "tears are a sign of
weakness" or 'boys don't cry." It is because of these messages
that so many have hit an emotional brick wall in adulthood and
ended up in therapy. It is amazing that we are never taught how
to manage our emotions, how to self-love, how to master our
own minds from early age. These are the most important life
skills that should be taught to our children in school.

Suppressing emotions is not healthy. There is a consequence
to every suppressed emotional trauma. Crying is essential to

resolving and processing grief and sadness. Suppressing, or even worse numbing these big emotions with addictions, often results in depression. It is essential to feel your emotions fully and completely. Feeling is healing! Once you feel all your emotions, you can move on and live with an open heart. Cry whenever you can, be thankful for having this superpower, and let your tears cleanse away your sadness and stress.

# Life Is a Balance of Holding On and Letting Go...

*You only lose what you cling to.* – Buddha

Sometimes the changes you fear are the changes you need the most. While growth is uncomfortable and painful, nothing can be more painful than the feeling of being stuck. As you grow up, you realize some weight needs to be left behind in order for the journey to get lighter. Most of us are master overthinkers. It is easy to get caught up in your own head and start overthinking life. Generally it's because you have unhealed parts of your soul that have been triggered. The best thing you can do in these situations is – let go!

Easier said than done? Of course it is, but it helps to understand at that particular low vibration you are not in a position of healthy judgment, and it's best not to attach labels to the situation. Holding on to pain or hurting someone else will not fix the situation. Wishing things were different will not change anything.

When you let go, you don't necessarily forget. You just let it be. As gracefully as you can, with much compassion, just let it be. Every time a thought arises, don't get involved in the drama of the mind, don't give it the satisfaction of overthinking. It will drain you without any resolution. Just like a nagging friend, listen to it and promptly tell it that you won't be participating in that conversation. Let it go.

Here are a few tips on how to let go:

☐ Consciously decide to let things go. Make a clear decision that the painful memory doesn't serve you and it's time to let it go.

☐ Give yourself permission to feel the sadness, anger, frustration, or whatever feeling you might have, fully and completely. Denying yourself the satisfaction to feel results in carrying unhealed emotional baggage. So if you are going to be sad, be really sad for a little bit. That will allow you to heal faster than suppressing the emotion.

☐ Practice daily gratitude. Make a list of everything you are grateful for and add to it daily.

☐ Change your scenery. Travel somewhere. It will help change your perspective.

☐ Love yourself completely. Forgive yourself for the past. Be compassionate with yourself and mindful of your self-talk. Be gentle, because after all, you are doing your best.

☐ Work with what you realistically have. Identify your present situation (emotional, financial, etc.) and make a list of things you can work with now. Try not to give in to painful memories or guilt about the past.

☐ Other releasing techniques include emotional clearings, energy healing, affirmations, mediation etc.

☐ Don't take life too seriously, and don't attach yourself to and be defined by people or things. After all, you can either grieve what you lost or be happy to be given the opportunity to experience life. Remain open to change. Be flexible so that you don't break. Enjoy this beautiful journey.

# Mirror, Mirror on the Wall...

*Despite how open, peaceful, and loving you*
*attempt to be, people can only meet you, as deeply*
*as they've met themselves.* – Matt Kahn

Your reality is a holographic reflection of you. Everything around you mirrors your thoughts and your vibes. Every single incident, interaction, and accident is a projection of YOU. How is it my fault, you might ask, if someone hits my car? Well it is not your fault; it is, however, a reflection of your current state of being. They say, "When it rains, it pours." It is exactly that! When you allow your vibration to lower based on a negative situation or incident, you invite more of that negativity into your reality. Hence, the accident or the traffic ticket on an already bad day mirrors the negative energy emanating from you.

Same is true for the opposite. When you wake up in a good mood and flow with the day in positive vibes, even work doesn't seem to be a hassle. No one can bring you down, and somehow you manage to bypass every negative situation by a miracle. This is flow! When you bring your vibration up, the entire universe conspires to guide you throughout your day and life flows effortlessly.

The trick is to stay tuned in to high vibrations. How can you do that you might wonder? Take a look at your reality and pay attention to your thoughts. How often are you angry? Resentful? Defensive? Cynical? Jealous? Do you thirst for revenge? If you allow such feelings to take root, they will poison you. If this is your pattern, then you most likely have mean and jealous people surrounding you ... or so you think, because people are only indicators of what is going on inside of you. You see people through your own programming. A person that seems kind to you may seem fake or rude to someone else, and it has nothing to do with that person. Similarly, people may all have different opinions of you, but it has nothing to do with you, and everything to do with their thoughts, their reality and perception.

Pay close attention to every situation and interaction. If you resist the temptation to point fingers outwards and only for a minute believe what you just read is true, you will start to see the patterns. This will help you make small changes towards elevating your vibration. And remember - self-love and self-care are crucial components in this process. Deliberately and consciously work the magic of the life-mirror to your advantage. Find what you want ...

- ☐ If you want to be loved, then LOVE
- ☐ If you want to be trusted, then TRUST
- ☐ If you are seeking peace, then FORGIVE
- ☐ To receive, then BE GRATEFUL
- ☐ If you need to be heard, then LISTEN
- ☐ And to be understood, then seek to UNDERSTAND!

Next time you look at your mirror of life, may you find only beauty. Remember, you are the master creator, so choose your thoughts and feelings wisely in order to create a life in which you can blossom.

# A Grateful Heart Is a Magnet for Miracles

*Anything that annoys you is teaching you patience.*
*Anyone who abandons you is teaching you*
*how to stand up on your own two feet.*
*Anything that angers you is teaching you*
*forgiveness and compassion.*
*Anything that has power over you is for teaching*
*you how to take your power back.*
*Anything you hate is teaching you unconditional love.*
*Anything you fear is teaching you courage to overcome your fear.*
*Anything you can't control is teaching you*
*how to let go and trust the Universe*
*– Jackson Kiddard*

What was the last time you said "thank-you" and really felt the gratitude tingles throughout your body? Here is an interesting theory about gratitude. The Universe always matches your vibration; so if you are in the gratitude vibration, the Universe is going to reward you with more of what you are grateful for. The Universe doesn't differentiate between good or bad, it reacts to the feeling and intention behind your thoughts and words. Be mindful of what you wish for, as it amplifies.

If you pay attention, you will notice that what you have today, or the situation you are in today or six months ago, is all a result of what you wished for yourself. If you are having a hard time seeing this now, stay tuned and you will see that everything is the result of your own thoughts and intentions. If you stay stuck in victim mentality, whining to everyone that your life is miserable and there is nothing positive about it, well guess what? You are never going to see anything positive around you. Whereas if you are grateful even in the darkest days, believing and keeping faith that whatever is happening now is not going to last forever, and affirm it is there to teach you to trust in the divine flow of life, which maybe your mind can't wrap itself around right now, then guess what? You will eventually see the light.

Every time you wish for something or ask the Universe / God to bring something to you, you put out a vibration of lack and scarcity. This means that the Universe is now going to have to shift things around, put you through a series of experiences so you can grow into a harmonious vibration of what you asked for. This takes time and if you are constantly asking for something you don't have, the process becomes never-ending and you never find yourself at peace. Instead you end up in ever-chasing mode. Try staying grateful for what's in front of you and feel the realities within. This way you can manifest your dreams and not chase them. When people argue about whether or not their cup is half full or half empty, be the person who is grateful to just have a cup!

Gratitude does not necessarily mean that you get excited at whatever occurs in your life. It is rather an awareness of what's in front of you. It is your willingness to allow flow to come into your life, without blocking or delaying the learning process whether the opportunity comes from fortune or misfortune.

Here are some gratitude tips to help you stay balanced

☐ Practice awareness of what's happening in your everyday physical reality. We spend so much time in our head listening to our Monkey Mind chatting about past or future, that we don't allow enough time to see what is here in the present. As Hellen Mellicost reminds us, when we live in the present moment, life is not hard.

☐ Always welcome the lessons. It is very difficult at times, when things seem very negative, with dark clouds hovering over your head and it is hard to see the beams of sunshine that are trying to break through them. When you find out you got laid off, it seems more like doors are closing rather than opening. It feels horrible, and it could annoy you to hear someone tell you, "Oh, but you will learn so much from this! Be grateful!" However, you really do need to stay focused, remain grateful, and have faith. Everything is in divine order.

☐ Let go of expectations and the need to control outcomes. Embrace the fact that nothing in your life has ever happened exactly as you planned for it, and nothing will probably ever happen that way. Set a goal, have faith, and let life take you there on its waves.

☐ Make a list of all the things for which you are grateful for ... but make sure you really feel each incident, item, feeling, and person. Don't just write a long list of stuff. Each day add at least 3 things that make you feel grateful. This is a powerful practice of training the mind to seek the positive in each and every situation. Don't underestimate its simplicity. When the mind is focused on gratitude it can't complain or create drama. Even if it seems really hard to stay grateful, identify simple things, like your health, the sun, the mattress that supports you while you sleep. As you keep doing this morning ritual, your list will take on more depths and layers. Stay consistent.

# Tune-In to Abundance Mindset

*Abundance is not something we acquire. It is something we tune into.* – Wayne Dyer

As a child you didn't have a concept of shortage. You believed anything was possible. Have you ever tried getting a six-year-old to rush and get ready for school? They don't understand why everyone is so frantic to get out of the house. When I tried rushing my son to school one day, he started stepping over dry Autumn leaves because they made a funny noise and he was curious. When you seem to be most in a rush, kids seem to have one more very important thing they need to do before getting into the car. How about explaining to the same child why you cannot purchase all the toys in the store for him/her. "What? You can't afford it? Why?"

You see, children come into this world with pure consciousness and abundant mindset - perfectly happy with the way they look, without financial worries or obligations, nowhere to rush, and they are very happy just playing. Through play they learn, imagine, and create. Because BEING is our natural state and DOING is what creates all the stress of life. Shortly after the child is born, however, we start unnecessary societal programming that creates resistance in children. As a child you have heard "No" and "Can't" so many times it slowly dimmed your limitless nature and forced you to believe in scarcity. Fitting in becomes the most important thing to pursue.

When did you start believing in scarcity? When you started associating everything with time and money. You see, I believe you come into this world with a mission and a budget, and you have work to do. But not the kind of work that makes you rush to work, hate your job, get exhausted, and leaves you empty. As a child everyone comes to this world with certain skills that dominate their personality/ability; however, we manage to fit every child into the same mold of public education and expect them all to come out the same. Well, what's the fun of that? Why spend 15-20 years of your life learning things and processes that you will end up spending another 10 years unlearning so you can connect with your purpose. The truth is, you already came with all the necessary knowledge and skills to accomplish your mission. Of course your life path will take you through a series of events to strengthen some skills, to learn some new ones, and to shed the unnecessary programming instilled by society.

Don't worry when you stumble on your learning path and make mistakes, wasting time and money, etc. That is all calculated into your budget. There is always enough of everything - money, time, resources - to accomplish your purpose. The minute you wake up to your purpose, everything will flow to you effortlessly and in an accelerated way. So quit thinking that you are running out of time or money, using those as excuses to stay in your scarce comfort zone. Push limits, follow what your heart decides, try new things, and allow life to unfold for you. Just take a breath and listen to your heart.

# Energy Is Our Currency

*Passion is energy. Feel the power that comes
from focusing on what excites you.*

\- Oprah Winfrey

You know the feeling when you feel strong, rested, accomplished, and inspired? Everything around you seems brighter. You feel happy, joyful and full of love. You can't stop smiling, people around you seem nicer, and even the little things that used to irritate you seem to have disappeared. This is you living from your power source! When your energy tank is full you willingly give to everyone, you radiate love, and you feel abundant in all areas of life. But when your energy level is low you tend to close off, get angry and irritable, and find yourself in unpleasant situations. The most important point to remember here is that it's not you - it's your energy level that you simply forgot to budget for correctly.

We talk about budgeting our money. We need to also budget our energy. Because when we have a lot of energy we are inspired, we are creative, we are ready to tackle the world, and we are very productive in that state. This in its turn can transfer into money, if that's what we want. Sounds easy enough?

So how do we budget our energy? You literally do only things that bring you joy! For me this meant switching from a TO DO calendar to a TO BE calendar for the month. I wrote out a test self-care calendar and decided to run my life around MY self-care, harnessing all the energy I could get. At the same time I minimized the work and commitments that didn't necessarily bring me joy. I took this project very seriously. I planned out each day starting at 5am and made sure to stuff my calendar with everything joyful, from yoga and massages to reading and spending time with friends/family, and everything in between. I intentionally made Mondays my self-care days to break the negative stigma of Mondays. It turned out when I did focus on work, I was actually much more effective and got more accomplished than when I forced myself to work when my tank was empty. No wonder so many countries are switching to shorter work weeks.

When you live your life by design, you don't mind giving from your overflow. You gladly serve your family and community with a smile on your face. Life hasn't dramatically changed for me. What changed was my attitude towards my life. I still run my business and take care of life tasks, but I no longer stress about it (mostly). I now do it with pleasure, because I learned to prioritize me, say no to what doesn't bring me joy, harness my energy, and channel it more effectively! I understand that sometimes life throws curveballs at you and you fall off the tracks. The trick is to just get back on the self-care wagon as soon as possible.

Cherish your energy by setting healthy boundaries. Find what fills your tank and make sure you do that routinely to keep vibrating at the higher level and staying elevated most of the time.

# Guiding Principle #3

*Starve Your Fears & Limiting Beliefs*

# Conquer Your Fears

*What if I fall? Oh, but my darling, what
if you fly?* - Erin Hanson

Let's talk about your fears and why they have so much power
over you. Fear is a projection of the illusions of your mind
into your reality. Fear is the limitation your mind sets towards
your actions. It is the perfect tool that your mind uses to
control you and keeps you in the safe comfort zone. The mind
doesn't like change and will find any excuse to make you feel
its pseudo "safety" by keeping you afraid. If you can just grasp
that you are NOT your mind, it will be easier to manage and
overcome fears. If you don't control your mind, it will be sure
to control you.

How can you overcome your fears? Start with making a list
of all the fears you have. Define them one by one. You can't
face something you can't identify. Write them down. This will
allow you to face your fears/demons and define them. Once
your fears have a name and you called them out, they will start
losing power over you

Focus on each one individually and ask yourself "What's
the obstacle? What's the monkey mind afraid of?" Really feel
your fear by visualizing yourself going through it. Play the
worst-case scenario without pausing at the scariest part, and
observe your body sensations. Do your shoulders tense up? Do

you feel tightness in your neck or back? Do your teeth clench? Do your hands sweat? Embrace the fear.

Now write down various solutions and ways you could conquer each fear. What would it take to get you to tip over to the other side and conquer it? Try to play it in your head again, but this time come to a safe conclusion. Start looking for three positives/blessings in these situations. Reflect on them and replace the fear scenario with the "best case scenario". Find the positive in each of those situations, no matter how hard it seems. If it is a criticism, quit focusing on that and instead find the positives to focus on and shift your attention toward it each time the criticism creeps up. There is always a silver lining

When you shift your focus from the problem to the solution, your mind gets rewired. Doing this consistently will train your mind to look for solutions instead of getting trapped in the rabbit hole of victim mentality. Growing up I told myself at all times, "When you think there is no way, there are at least five different ways that you haven't thought about! Find them." Once you say this statement, your mind will immediately go to work and, trust me, it will find them.

If the fear is too big, try breaking it down into bite-size, manageable pieces. Start small and grow the expertise. Reward yourself for trying and give yourself plenty of credit for even the smallest step. Be gentle with yourself. You are doing your best.

Find the will to tip over the edge and just do it. Once you set your mind on doing it, you might just believe that you can.

Remember that it is ALL in your mind. In reality, unless

there is an immediate physical threat to your body, you will always be safe. The limit is in the mind led by the ego. Conquering fears is very liberating. It gives a sense of great accomplishment, gets you closer to your true self, and inspires you to live life fearlessly. Each victory will give you the courage to move on to conquering the next fear, and your courage will grow exponentially. Beliefs can be changed, but only if you embrace your fear.

So next time you get an opportunity to speak in public, zip line, express your opinion, chat up the guy/girl at the coffee shop, just go for it! Slowly but surely your bite-size fears will grow to become your confidence, and all the butterflies in your stomach will fly away, or at least fly in formation.

# Restructure Your Beliefs to Create the Life You Want

*Whether you think you can or whether you think you can't, you're right.* – Henry Ford

Belief is an illusion, yet it has so much power over us. A belief system is acquired knowledge, and beliefs only live in your head. This is good and bad at the same time. It is bad because all of us have dysfunctional and limiting beliefs that don't serve us and hinder our growth. Yet it is empowering to know that by simply shifting a simple belief, we can gain our power back.

Try this. Pick a limiting belief that you have, such as "I can never … (plug a word/phrase here)" and replace this with "I can … (plug the same word/phrase)." Pay attention to how your body feels when you pronounce each one of these several times. If you repeat anything a number of times, it registers in your subconscious mind as a belief, and soon enough it becomes your reality.

Have you noticed how hard is it to argue with people about things in which they believe strongly? Core beliefs get formulated through extensive programming starting from childhood, influenced by parents, educational systems, religion, society, media, and so on. If enough of these channels feed into the same idea, it slowly registers in your subconscious mind as a belief. Your mind, in its turn, starts looking for more validation to support that which then over time becomes a core belief. (Read *Open Your Heart to Settle Your Mind* in Section 4). If the belief is not questioned over time, and enough people around you propagate the same belief, then you can be convinced it is the truth and nothing but the truth. But wait, there is more. Many beliefs have been transferred to us from several previous generations, which were influenced by living conditions and limited knowledge available to our ancestors. I call it the collective consciousness, which is easy to identify in clichés and superstitions, such as "money is the root of all evil."

When someone brings up their opinion about something and you find yourself strongly disagreeing, remember it is their belief. You don't have to agree, but you also cannot judge. It simply differs from your belief. If we consider how each and every one of us has been raised in different cultures, educational systems, and societal conditions, then whose beliefs are really right? Depending on where I am in different parts of the country or the world, majority beliefs change dramatically. Unless I want to conform, I am left with no choice but to question. Extensive questioning of my own personal beliefs as a foreigner led me to understand that beliefs are simply illusions, they are not universal truths. If enough people understood this in the world, we would have more peace.

To identify your limiting beliefs, ask yourself "where am I stuck in my life?" Or "which beliefs don't work for me any longer?" Maybe you believe you don't deserve to be loved because you are not pretty, etc. Pay attention to your self-talk.

Is it positive or do you often put yourself down over very minor "failures"? (Read *The Art of Self-Care* in Section 4).

Dysfunctional beliefs can be disguised in very simple thought patterns, such as "I always get sick before a big event" or "I am shy" or "I can never get anything right the first time." These may have been your reality for your entire lifetime so far, but once you bring awareness to these beliefs and set the intention to release and replace them with new and positive beliefs, you can change your life.

Some beliefs may take longer to break. Many are wired by habits, and it may take a few times of falling into the old pattern to release the belief completely, but don't get discouraged. Give it some time. Be especially mindful of anything that comes after "I am ..." and "You are ..." Make sure to switch to a positive statement each time you first mention something negative. Set an intention to shift and do the work.

Life can be a breeze if you have the right tools. So next time you catch yourself with a dysfunctional belief, pause, intentionally replace it with a positive belief that serves your highest and best interests, and watch the miracles unfold.

# Follow Your Passion Blindly – You ARE Enough

*When perfectionism is driving, shame is riding shotgun, and fear is that annoying backseat driver.* – Brené Brown

Perfectionism can kill your dreams! How many times have you stopped doing something because it wasn't perfect, because you were ashamed or got scared of public judgment? When I was a kid I loved the stage. I'd dance, play in theatre, and sing my heart out. I wasn't that great at these, but no one was about to stop me from getting on stage and having a blast. Most of the time I would make a fool of myself, but I couldn't care less. I liked to be center stage and loved the attention of the audience, plus there were always those who cheered on my courage and energy. I never doubted myself or occupied myself with other people's opinions. I was too busy being me.

So when did we decide that we are NOT enough? As we grow up and reach our teens, the societal norms and opinions get deep under our skin and start corroding our teenage self-esteem and push us into their boxes of values and morals. As young adults we start appealing to public reactions and loose our authenticity. Pair this up with being pushed to become overachievers and to constantly compare and compete in every aspect of our lives, and it creates the perfect production machine that can always be improved. No wonder the society today is so sensitive to public opinion and constantly tries to "keep up with the Jones."

If you are trapped in the "not good enough" blame game, take a breath and pause. You are exactly where you need to be and you are perfect with all your imperfections. Here are a few steps to take when your trickster mind tries to devalue your worth.

1. The first step is focusing on self-love and changing the inner dialogue. You can't become successful if you keep reminding yourself what a failure you are. Be compassionate and loving to yourself and reward yourself for trying. Each time you criticize yourself, stop and find at least three things you love about yourself, and each time come up with something new. Slowly you will notice there are more things that are good about you than bad.

2. Focus on the progress instead of the perfection. Take a look at your life's journey and notice how far you've come. Almost always you will see you have progressed one way or another. It may not have been according to your plan, but nevertheless you are here, and probably farther along than you thought you could go.

3. Stop comparing yourself to anyone else. Everyone has their journey and their karma, and you don't need to get involved in other people's business. Everyone goes

through struggles, so mind you own life and make the best of it. Keep your focus on your goals.

4. Make peace with your current situation. Until you understand this, you will keep chasing life and never feel satisfied. You've been dealt cards, so learn to play them and make the best of it. Only then will you progress to the next level of this ultimate game called Life. It is not a linear journey, it's a spiral replay where you can only graduate and move up if you learn to master the level you are in right now.

Now that I think about it, if I kept on doing the things I loved as a child with the same fearless attitude and passion, who knows. I could have become a Hollywood actress by now.

What are you holding back from because of fears of shame or judgment? Now imagine how far you could go if you believed that you are enough.

# You Can't Do Life Alone

*When you hand good people possibility,*
*they do great things.* – Biz Stone

There is a reason we are each born with various talents and passions. Some of us are well versed in creative work while others are great at structure. This is because we came to this world with different purposes, none any less important than the other. We are all connected – like a watch mechanism that is built with a million pieces, yet none can function without the other. Each and every piece is essential to the entire operation.

For better or for worse, we grew up in a system that pushed for multitasking, encouraging us to be very individualistic and extremely competitive. We tend to use the word 'team work" in almost every area of our life; however, a close observation reveals that most of our societal roles, at school, work, family, and even with friends, reward competitiveness rather than teamwork. Our parents always wanted us to be better, push harder, and get the medals and honors regardless whether we liked doing what we were put into or not. As a result we grew up so disconnected with ourselves that we can't even find our true passion, focus on the one thing that makes us happy, and most importantly, trust others to do what they are good at.

Being an overachiever myself, I tend to take on more tasks at a given time than I can emotionally handle. Physically – no problem. I can champion through them all, as I was raised to multitask and overachieve. The problem is it takes a toll on me emotionally. I learned that spending too much time doing (working) and not enough time being (caring for self, disconnecting, pausing) drains me and allows anxiety and stress to creep in very quickly.

Additionally, many of us are perfectionists one way or another, which can express itself in a multitude of ways – from "OCD" behavioral patterns, meticulousness, or taking up a task and dropping it just as quickly. I remember when I opened The Salt Room, I spent so much time overthinking every single detail, from branding and merchandising to baseboard colors. This got to the point where I had to hire a designer to match the color of the walls to the unique color of baseboards. I know, you are probably thinking I am crazy. But at that time, my mind couldn't rest and move on until I had figured out that color issue. Even when my general manager Tammy came on board, I had a hard time letting go of control. I would show her how to do something very simple, then catch myself saying "It's OK, I'll do it." Talk about a crazy perfectionist.

Slowly I learned to let go of control and to increase my level of trust. Soon enough I realized that people actually all have different talents. My job isn't to teach them how to do something in which they have no interest. Rather, my job is to find the experts in the fields where I need help and trust they will do a better job than I will, since it is their passion. To my surprise, Tammy actually ended up doing things a lot better and more efficiently than I could ever have imagined. What a liberating feeling to know that I don't have to do everything. I learned to delegate and trust, which opened up a whole new world of creativity for me. I now have time to develop and implement new ideas, which is my passion, and allow others to help me co-create. Even when things don't turn out the way I want them to, I have learned to understand human error and be encouraging of growth. After all, I have made a few mistakes myself getting here.

It is almost always worth allowing experts to do the work about which they are passionate. There is a level of empowerment in just that. Magic happens when co-creation is in process, when everyone does what they are great at and you trust them to do their job. Learn to identify your strengths as well as others' strengths, and then delegate/distribute the tasks accordingly. Everyone will have more fun doing their work, and it will get done much more efficiently than if you were to do it all alone.

# The Only Way to It, Is Through It

*The best way out is always through.* - Robert Frost

They say we come to this world for growing our souls through lessons and experiences. That makes Life merely a replay of the same movie. Has it ever occurred to you that you tend to repeat certain patterns throughout your lifetime? While scenarios and people may be different in any given episode, the situation and the feelings are the same, which is what confirms you are stuck in the old pattern. Most people live their lives unconsciously thinking that these patterns are simply the way their life is meant to be. They blame it on life itself or on others for what's happening to them. You'll hear them say "That's just how my life has always been," or "Everyone always takes advantage of me." These people fail to recognize the patterns and understand that change is in their hands. It may have always been that way, but it doesn't have to be anymore if you choose to take action now.

I have always struggled with setting healthy boundaries and somehow always found myself feeling taken advantage of. At first I thought people are just greedy or selfish and I am too kind. It took me nearly 30 years to understand there is nothing wrong with people. I simply did not know how to set healthy boundaries or that there is no need to please people to be loved. This one seemingly simple realization brought such peace into my life. All of a sudden people stopped being greedy or selfish, and I did not feel any urge to please anyone anymore.

Next time you find yourself in a repeating pattern - bad relationship, work conflict, friendship issues, etc. - pause and focus on the feeling. If it feels familiar, ask yourself "What do I need to learn to not feel this way anymore?" The answer will come to you without you trying too hard. When it comes, you'll know. By replaying the movie you get to grow your soul. You learn little details, you have ah ha moments. Unfortunately, even when you recognize the situation and try to skip the lesson by not getting involved, it tends to circle back and find you again. The only way to it is through it. Once you fully learn your lesson, the episode leaves your journey for good and the pattern stops.

# Breaking the Chains of Codependency

*You are not being mean when you say NO to unreasonable demands or when you express your ideas, feelings, and opinions, even if they differ from those of others.*– Beverly Engel

Are you Facebook happy or are you genuinely happy with your life? Do you know the difference? Take a look at your relationships with your husband/wife, boyfriend/girlfriend, children, family, and friends. Do you dedicate yourself fully to their happiness, yet complain that you never have time for yourself and it is their fault? The majority of families in the generations prior to this one lived in codependent relationships. The only difference is that back then divorce was shamed, so people would tolerate dysfunctional unions. Now they just move to the next union without fixing the dysfunction.

Codependent people take too much responsibility for other people's emotions and feelings, and it is not healthy. But how can being giving be a bad thing you might think? It is actually a major disservice to those with whom you have a relationship when you go along with whatever the other one wants and you feel resentful and unfulfilled.

Here are some hidden issues behind codependent behavior:

☐ People pleasing / low self-esteem / need for validation

☐ Fear of being rejected / alone

☐ Inability to communicate your needs and set healthy boundaries

As you know, the first step to recovery is admitting you have a problem. Here is your wake-up call – you have a problem! Second step is to figure out what YOU want in any given situation. It seems quite simple, but most people have a hard time figuring it out. "Whatever you want," was my response pattern to almost every question. This is a very dangerous habit, because all of us have wants, and we need to learn how to access them, honor them, and get them met in a healthy way.

Of course we have a hard time knowing what we want. Generally we grow up conditioned by our parents, who get to decide what we eat, how much of it, what we wear, and most of us haven't been given much choice in anything. Then when you grow up and get married, you start catering to the needs of your family. I personally had a hard time answering the question about what I wanted for breakfast. I had no idea how I liked my eggs, as I always prepared breakfast for others, and sort of ended up eating whatever was available. In ten years of a committed relationship I never made a meal for myself. It took me almost three years after my separation to start getting to know myself. That was an extensive time of self-care, traveling, and trying out new things. The key out of codependency is to get into creating a life you love and not giving up your habits for anyone. Coexist, don't codepend.

# Guiding Principle #4

*Embrace Love as You
Chase Your Dreams*

# The Art of Self-Care

*Almost anything will work again if you unplug it for
a few minutes, including you.* - Anne Lamott

Throughout our lives we are programmed to care for everyone
else but ourselves. We are kind, compassionate, and generous
to everyone, but when the time comes to do all of that for
ourselves, a sense of guilt and self-judgment takes over us.

Self-care is NOT selfish. It is integral to healing. By practicing
self-care and learning to extend love toward yourself, you begin
to cultivate feelings of self-worth, strength, and resiliency,
leaving behind self-abuse and harmful coping mechanisms you
may have used to mask negative feelings about yourself.

Self-care is important to living a balanced life because it
helps you become more mindful of your thoughts, behaviors,
and actions. When you love yourself, your love tank is full and
you can give from your overflow.

It shouldn't be difficult. Simply take time to do what you
love! At times, we are so busy pleasing everyone else that we
even forget what we love. Spend some time with yourself, get
to know you, and start putting your needs first.

Here are a few tips on how to self-care:

☐ Meditation and/or yoga
☐ Reading

☐ Socializing with friends

☐ Arts – drawing, dancing, singing, or simply listening to music

☐ Spending time in solitude in nature

These are simply suggestions. Think about what self-care looks like for you. Create a self-care calendar and fill it with all the things that bring you joy, leaving almost no room for distraction. Keep busy loving yourself and cultivating the perfect life that you want to live. Create a bucket list; make weekly, monthly, quarterly, and yearly goals that you look forward to; and take it very seriously. Here is what my self-care routine looked like:

✓ 5am - wake up, meditation, prayers and affirmations

✓ 5:40 - drive to a yoga class and listen to one TEDx talk or Audible chapter

✓ 6am - yoga (min 3 times a week)

✓ 7:30am - shower

✓ 8am get ready for the day.

✓ Evening reflection, visualization

- Mondays off - spend the day self-caring (choice of massage, facial, energy healing, staying home, listening to classical music and reading, journaling, driving to the mountains, watching a movie, spending time with friends and family, etc.)

- Weekly - Make minimum 2-3 business connections, and connect with minimum 1-2 friends. Spend at least one day alone.
- Monthly - Do something I have never done before. Read 1-2 books per month.
- Yearly - attend a growth conference or seminar, travel for leisure 3-4 times and visit a new place I have never been before, attend at least 3 concerts and/or cultural events.

I plugged in events and activities throughout the week that made me happy. I would sign up for things or make arrangements to meet with people I wanted to spend time with. I worked my self-care schedule to make business meetings possible. Therefore, when it was time to work, I did so with great pleasure, passion and incredible effectiveness.

I would lie to you if I said I kept the scales balanced throughout the entire year. Of course at times of growth and busy seasons, this calendar would take a back seat. Just knowing what I knew already, I could bring it right back and make self-care a priority.

# Love Is an Inside Job

*In the realm of love, a paradox exists: you can effectively love others only when you can love yourself.* - Gay Hendricks

Let's talk about love. Generally, every person has their own unwritten definition of Love, which is why Gary Chapman came up with five love languages to help educate on various ways people give and receive love. When you Google the definition of Love as a verb, you get - "feel a deep romantic or sexual attachment to (someone)." Romantic or sexual attachment? Seriously? No wonder people are stuck in unhealthy codependent relationships.

Love is so much more multidimensional than this petty definition. The power of love is limitless. - Love can heal, Love can end wars, Love can save and liberate, Love can inspire and empower, Love spreads compassion and sets you free. Love can open doors to endless possibilities. Love is not just sexual, it's not infatuation, it's not lust. Love cannot be bought or sold, forced, or taken away. Love doesn't condition or judge. Love is bigger than you. Love is the most profound emotion you can experience as a human.

Most importantly, love starts with you. It's an inside job. Self-love is the missing link to fully understanding the concept of love. Unconditional love is your birthright. Unfortunately, many of us can't define for ourselves what it means, so we expect others to provide us with that feeling of safety and love. You tend to demand from others what you cannot give to yourself. It is not fair to place such a burden on people around you, because no matter how much love they give you, it will never be enough. So learn your own love language and fulfill it yourself before you have someone else fill your love tank.

You get love by giving it, and you can't give it if you don't have it. It's a beautiful cycle and a fine balancing act. Here are a few tips to help you start your journey to self-love:

1. Write five things every day that you absolutely love about yourself, then affirm them and own the awesome person that you are!

2. Practice forgiveness and self-compassion. Forgive yourself for everything you have presumably done wrong in the past. Be gentle with yourself ... you are doing your best. Forgive others, as everyone acts out simply from their own lack of self-love.

3. Feel your emotions. Let go of numbing habits, such as excessive shopping, eating, drugs, sex, drinking, etc. Allow yourself to feel the pain, and be compassionate to yourself. The only way to it is through it. It helps reminding yourself that the destructive habit is not going to fix the situation each time you are pulled to engage in it.

4. Practice the art of self-care. (See *The Art of Self-Care* above). Do the things that spark joy in your soul. Love

yourself unconditionally and unapologetically, just the way you are.

5. Detox from judgment - judgment of self and judgment towards others. Every time your mind judges, pause and see the beauty in the person or situation. Remove yourself from toxic situations and people. Detox from anything that brings judgment into your life. Consciously focusing on the positive will help rewire your brain in a very short time. You can't afford even a single negative thought. You need to "cultivate the rose garden of your mind" as the monk said from *The Monk that Sold His Ferrari.* Don't judge yourself if you slip.

Unconditional love for self will open up endless possibilities for you. Fill your love tank so much that you cannot help but spread love and kindness all around you. Try to see beauty in everything and everyone, even if it is hard to see. Be the spark that warms up people's hearts.

Remember you are a divine being who is having a human experience. You are simply here to walk the journey, have a series of experiences, and complete a mission. Don't beat yourself up over things that are out of your control and stay clear of programming and comparing. Your job is to discover your gifts and share them with the world.

# Open Your Heart to Settle Your Mind

*If we learn to open our hearts, anyone, including the people who drive us crazy, can be our teacher.* ~Pema Chodron

Overthinking is your straight shot to nowhere because it only happens in your mind. And your mind is a convincing liar and can be a very dark place at times. It sure has a lot of twists and turns and it loves drama; so it puts together some puzzle pieces by plugging in years-old information and programming to create the perfect case, which it then uses to defend your ego all on its own.

This vicious cycle can go on forever, considering that you are always going to add bits and pieces of information (aka puzzle pieces) trying to perfect your case. Each time you revisit your case, your heart beats faster, anger and anxiety take over, and you get out of breath. This is an extremely dangerous spiral downward as this can take years of your life and incredible amounts of energy. (See *Energy Is Our Currency* in Section 2). The longer you stay in the depths of your mind, the more you alienate from your heart, which is where the settlement of the case resides.

Instead, implement these techniques to help open up your heart and settle the case of the mind:

1. Pause … Breathe through each tension, anger trigger, anxiety attack … Simply take 5-10 slow deep conscious belly breaths. You will instantly feel more peaceful.

2. Meditate 20 minutes a day - EVERY DAY. Learn various techniques - transcendental meditation, visualization meditation, contemplation meditation, relaxation meditation, etc. There are plenty of techniques. Or simply sit with your eyes closed, check with your body slowly starting with your toes, all the way to the crown of your head, wrapping yourself in a bright golden white light. Sometimes I call a conference meeting between my spirit guides, angels, archangels, ancestors, and my higher self where I simply ask them to give me a message or tell me something I need to know. Remember, all the answers you are searching for reside within you. You just need to silence your mind and ask for guidance.

3. Ask yourself, "What else is possible with this person/situation?" or "How can this get any better?" You may not have an instant response in your head, but keep this question in mind each time you find yourself overthinking the same scenario. And remember, there is always another perspective, another resolution to each and every situation. The challenge is it may be hard to see the alternative when your mind will only feed you the familiar tunnel vision story.

4. If possible, communicate. Open a door. Start a conversation, any kind of conversation, then listen

actively with an open mind and open heart. People tend to share a lot of information through their body language, eye contact, use of words, and energy. Observe with curiosity.

5. Refrain from interrupting or jumping to conclusions. If something is unclear, don't fall back into your default state of overthinking to validate your case. Instead, ask clarifying questions.

6. Most importantly communicate from your heart. Don't be scared to share your feelings and be vulnerable. There is a lot of healing from this alone.

Most of the time what you think is happening around you or what you think other people think is far from the truth. The overthinking is caused by insecurities, old trauma triggers, as well as life programming. Each person formulates his or her own case based on their own programming, which has nothing to do with you or your version of the case. Communication from the heart opens doors to healing and settling unresolved cases. It bridges the gap and dissolves boundaries, making us one again. So the next time you find yourself in the downward spiral of the mind, connect with your heart.

# If $Money$ Wasn't an Issue
# What Would You Be Doing?

*Money is numbers and numbers never end. If it takes money to be happy, your search for happiness will never end.* - Bob Marley

Everybody seems so busy these days, running towards some imaginary destination that can't be defined. Many of us live in the future in our minds, while trapped physically in this never-ending rat race. How many times have you caught yourself saying, "I will do what I like once I make X amount of money," or "I will take care of myself when I have more time," or "I will live my dream life in X amount of years, after _____." These are just a few examples of how you lie to yourself daily.

I remember when I was in college barely making ends meet, I told myself, "If I can just make an extra $200 a month I'll be good!" Then when I graduated and started working, the script changed. "If I could only make an extra $1000 a month I will be financially free." This went on until I started making a six-figure salary and realized how unhappy I was. Money was NOT going to fix it. Sound familiar?

Are you too busy to do the things you love? Do you even know what you love at this point? I challenge you to put your life on pause, pull out a blank sheet of paper, and write this down: ***How would I live my life if I had unlimited time and money?*** See what comes up and write everything down.

Before you start jumping into giving me the cliché "I would live in a castle with a prince/princess" or "I would travel the world" or "I would just do nothing," I challenge you to pause again and imagine what that really looks like. Not for a month, not for a year, but forever. Can you tell me what your daily life would look like after you got all the superficial dreams out of your system; like buying an island and laying on the beach for days on end, or waking up every day in a different country (which by the way can be somewhat tiring and make you homesick). No matter what you did, sooner or later you would circle right back into a dysfunctional pattern of misery and something would always be missing, until you were ready to do the work.

You see, no amount of money in the world can bring you closer to yourself. No matter how far you travel you can't run away from yourself, and no matter which prince charming you marry, you will never be happy if you haven't met and learned to love yourself.

So now on that blank sheet of paper, write down what your ideal day, week, month, year looks like if you didn't have any time or money restraints. Chances are you have plenty of time and money right now to do a lot on your list that makes you genuinely happy, but you simply never made yourself and your desires a priority!

# The Sky Is the Limit

*The sky is not the limit, your mind is.* - Marilyn Monroe

I asked my seven-year-old son Ethan if I could buy his cheeks, how much would he sell them to me for, and he said, without hesitation, $100,000 dollars. Then I asked what would he do with $100,000 dollars? Of course, he said he'd go spend it all on toys. Could you imagine how much fun Ethan would have spending $100K on toys? Do you think he would be thinking about running out of money? Or that he'd never have a chance to get more money? No. He'd spend it down to a penny and ask for another toy tomorrow. And guess what, the Universe would provide him with more. Somehow, somewhere, we would come across a friend or relative who would gladly get him the toy of his liking for some odd occasion.

So why are humans so worried about not having enough money? From where did this scarcity mentality come? You see, we were all programmed into scarcity mentality. All of our money-saving values and beliefs were generationally instilled in our DNA from ancestors who lived through war, poverty, famine, and God knows what else. These values come from collective generational programming. We don't even understand how lucky and blessed we are to be living in this generation. This lifetime is abundant. Most everyone on the planet is safe on a daily basis, and there is more than enough for everyone.

Yet our mind traps us into this scarcity mentality of lack and the need for more to feel safe and comfortable. Of course our consumer driven culture plays a big role in this mindset.

The difference between Ethan spending the 100K and you spending the 100K on something that you absolutely love is the feeling of scarcity, spender's remorse, the guilt of blowing your last penny on fun instead of responsibility, and the fear of not having enough for tomorrow. All of this is incomprehensible in a child's pure consciousness which has not yet been programmed by scarcity and instilled with fear. Those exact feelings are the ones blocking you from receiving more from the Universe. If you could slowly train your mind to tune into 'deserve' program vs. 'scarcity' program, you would slowly get the toxic feelings of fear, guilt, and remorse out of you. When you train your mind on abundance as opposed to scarcity, you are ready to manifest all your wishes into your life.

Now don't go blowing it all tomorrow because you're not ready yet. Start small:

1. Say "Thank you" and "I deserve it" and build the feeling up slowly. Spend money on things you love, reward yourself for little things. Lots of self-care and self-love is key.
2. Lift the limiting belief around money, block negative emotions of guilt, remorse, etc. and start feeling comfortable around abundance.

3. Live the life you'd want to live if you had more resources within your current affordability. From the moment you wake up do exactly what you would want to be doing throughout the day if you had enough money. Just use your imagination to fill the gaps.

4. When making a decision around spending, don't base it solely on lack of resources. Consider other factors, such as quality, intention, or whether the purchase aligns with your core values.

5. Finally, if it makes you happy and brings you joy, do it. You deserve it!

The sky is the limit. The Universe is abundant. The number of zeroes is irrelevant. It's about getting comfortable around abundance, learning to receive with pleasure, tuning into the positive feelings, and owning the confidence around whatever lifestyle you want. When you lift your limitations and flow with it, the Universe simply provides. So be thankful for the opportunities that come across your path and be open enough to receive unlimited abundance.

# Conclusion

In conclusion I would like to remind you: *You are a divine being and you get to command your own Universe.* You are exactly where you need to be and you are enough. Just get out of your own way and stop labeling your actions with judgment. When you remove your limiting beliefs, old programming from your culture/parents/school, and shed anything that doesn't serve you, you are left with your pure essence. This pure essence knows exactly what it wants and where it's going - without judgment, without fear, with a clear mind and a strong purpose.

Once you align with your purpose and find what it is that your soul wants, which requires silencing your mind, the journey becomes effortless. You allow things to unfold, refusing to get caught up in your current circumstances and seeing things from a higher perspective. At that time, life simply becomes a beautiful movie with a series of events that connect together, with emotions that fuel your journey, and in the end, when you look back, everything starts making perfect sense. You finally realize that everything is in divine order! Life is a journey, and healing is simple if you use the right tools, trust the people that come to help you, and open up to the opportunities that come to help you grow your soul.

Whatever you want is already yours, otherwise you wouldn't want it. Trust that what you genuinely want and gravitate to is exactly what is meant for you. The Universe is abundant and limitless. Not everybody wants a Mercedes after all. Believe you deserve it, remove the obstacles and limiting beliefs, get out of your own way, and let it unfold for you. Let the Universe guide you into the flow, and remember that you are always on time, always protected, always taken care of, and most of all, always loved.

In the end, there is only LOVE and LOVE is all you need. It's when you distance yourself from love that the fear takes over. Fear is simply lack of self-love. Every moment of every day you have a choice, and the choice only comes down to love or fear. Every decision you make is wired with either love (compassion, care, win-win) or fear (fear of judgment, criticism, shame, lack, vulnerability). Fear can only be conquered with more love. Only through loving yourself more and respecting your personal boundaries can you conquer your fears and spread light. Once you embrace this, your heart will open for light to enter and Love will flow through your veins like life-force, nourishing every cell of your body. Be the light that spreads love ...

# Afterword

*(Written in May, 2020 during the COVID-19 Lockdown)*

As the world comes to a standstill I wonder ... Being stuck at home may not necessarily be so bad after all. When productivity overruns your purpose, the Universe finds a way to slow you down so consciousness can find its way to sneak in. You become more aware of your thoughts, you connect more with those that matter, and you see life in a whole new perspective ... one that actually matters. You re-evaluate your priorities and start questioning:

What have I done so far and what am I really supposed to do in life?

When did the accomplished feeling of doing more replace the simple joys of life?

When you are separated from your titles and positions, when you can no longer be associated with certain groups or impress others, when your productive routine is no longer running your life, and even when a beauty and fashion regiment is no longer accessible, what are you left with? Look in the mirror and be honest with yourself. Do you like the person that's staring back at you? Are you proud of him or her? Have you managed to create a life routine that brings you joy or were you too busy being busy, chasing money and titles to impress people that do not matter? Have you taken for granted the ones that actually do NEED and DESERVE your time and attention?

Stay still…

Everything is always in divine order, whether you think so or not, whether you like it or not. You only have control over your reaction and your choices. Nothing else is under your control. Just breathe and flow; no judgment, no anxiety, just flow. The COVID-19 crisis gave us all a perfect opportunity to reflect on our lives. Being able to stay still in quarantine for two months forced us to pause, pivot, and reset. It allowed us to dream again, to connect with what really makes us happy, to re-evaluate relationships we have with people. It allowed us to see that time and money are not what matters.

I recall saying "If only I had the time, I'd clean up my car interior until it was sparkly clean." A month into lock down that car hadn't been touched. It made me wonder. Now I understand that time was never the issue. It is Energy we are after – that feeling that sparks joy and fuels action. But it is hard sometimes to connect with that feeling during inaction, when our mind is blocked and our heart is heavy. It helps to prioritize and act on things that get stuff done, and the joy will follow. When fear runs the mind, it goes into a block or overthinking mode, which in its turn drains our energy. We start giving in to procrastination and laziness and disruptive habits slowly creep in.

It's important to understand that it's OK to slow down, it is even OK to fall off the tracks, and maybe indulge a little more than usual considering the circumstances of being on lock down. Be gentle and try not to judge yourself. You are still human and balance is a skill that takes a lifetime to master. Just try not to allow this to become a habit. Snap out of it as soon as possible, because whatever you do for a long period of time becomes a habit, which then turns into a lifestyle. We all know how much more difficult it can be to reverse habits and change life styles.

So start today and pay attention to all the small choices you make or don't make throughout the day, because each step is a choice. Inaction is actually a choice. Ask yourself whether that choice is in line with your standards of integrity, whether it makes you proud of the person you are, whether it aligns with your long-term goals. There are only two choices – love or fear – and the choice is yours. Remember, fear is an illusion created by your mind to keep you safe in your comfort zone, so choose LOVE every time, even if it scares you!

Thank you COVID-19 for all your lessons and blessings…

# Acknowledgments

They say it takes a village to raise a child. I feel as if in my case it took several villages. I would like to thank each and every person that has ever crossed my path, as it is through all of you collectively that I came to learn and grow into the person I am today. I am especially grateful to the ones that played pivotal roles in my life in teaching and influencing me, in breaking and shaping me, in healing and nurturing me through the phases of my life; especially those who have always loved me and stood by me through all of it. My mother Tamara Tonoyan, who taught me resilience and shaped me into an independent woman, my ex-husband who gave me the best gift I could ever ask for - my amazing son Ethan - and thanks to whom I learned how to stand on my own two feet and claim my worth.

I am grateful for my family who is a gift from God and always stands by me when I need a shoulder to lean on. I am grateful to my spiritual mentors who were sent to me at very strategic times in my life: Betty Jones who taught me meditation, Claudia Gallo, Deborah Veach, Ronnie Tice and all my earth angels and fairy healers. You helped me through my difficult times and shed light on my situation so I could keep the faith.

I am grateful for my friends, new and old, who supported me in all of my crazy decisions, held space for me when I should have seen a therapist, stepped up to help when my business was on the brink of closure, and stuck it out with me through it all. To name a few: Tamara Gaboyan for being the pillar of my business and my best friend; Elena Ledoux for embracing me like family from the moment she met me and being determined to move me out of surviving and into thriving within a matter of months. I am grateful to all the wonderful women in the Las Vegas community who helped spread the word and grow my business, nominated me for awards when I did not feel very award-worthy, and provided me with platforms to express my voice. Each and every one of you has a special place in my heart and helped me see the light when I felt darkness all around me.

I am grateful to my staff for truly embracing the core values of my business and taking care of our clients like they would take care of their family. I am grateful to all my clients who always support me in every crazy endeavor and novelty I throw at them. I am so incredibly grateful to the entire Las Vegas Community, especially all the empowered women who inspire me every day to be kinder, more compassionate, more generous, and more supportive. I have never met such a small community in such a large city (and I come from a small country) that stands by each other and supports each other like one big family. It truly feels like a small town where the farmer still trades milk for bread from the local baker. My business has more supporters, promoters, and ambassadors than I could ask for. I am so grateful to each and every one of them.

I am forever grateful to my editor, Cindy Clemens. It is thanks to her that this book came to life. Cindy inspired me to share this with the world and gently moved me forward on this project despite my shifting priorities in life. When she first read my blogs, she told me, "My dear, you have a voice! People need to hear what you have to say!" A big shout out to Claudia Kuzniak for putting on the final polish and line edit so my voice would be truly heard. Special thank you to my book photographer Ati Grinspun, who was able to translate my soul and true happiness through pictures.

This seems surreal and I feel deep gratitude in every cell of my body.

Printed in the United States
By Bookmasters